Contents

Some words are shown in bold, **like this**. You can find out what they mean by looking in the glossary.

Meet the dogs

Do you have a dog? Or maybe you wish you could have one? Dogs can be good fun to take for walks and play with. People who have a pet dog enjoy the animal's company, and the dog can help them stay happy and healthy. But there is so much more to a dog than being a pet.

Many dogs love to play physical games with their owners.

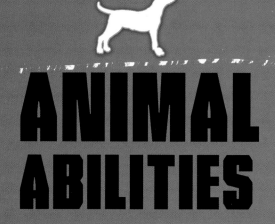

ANIMAL ABILITIES

DOGS

Charlotte Guillain

Raintree is an imprint of Capstone Global Library Limited, a company incorporated in England and Wales having its registered office at 7 Pilgrim Street, London, EC4V 6LB – Registered company number: 6695582

www.raintreepublishers.co.uk
myorders@raintreepublishers.co.uk

Edited by Laura Knowles, Abby Colich, and Diyan Leake
Designed by Victoria Allen and Ken Vail Graphic Design
Original illustrations © Capstone Global Library Ltd 2013
Illustrated by HL Studios
Picture research by Elizabeth Alexander
Originated by Capstone Global Library Ltd
Printed and bound in China by CTPS

ISBN 978 1 406 25909 4 (hardback)
17 16 15 14 13
10 9 8 7 6 5 4 3 2 1

ISBN 978 1 406 25916 2 (paperback)
18 17 16 15 14
10 9 8 7 6 5 4 3 2 1

British Library Cataloguing in Publication Data
Guillain, Charlotte.
    Dogs. -- (Animal abilities)
    1. Dogs--Juvenile literature. 2. Animal intelligence--Juvenile literature.
    I. Title II. Series
    636.7-dc23

Acknowledgements
We would like to thank the following for permission to reproduce photographs: Alamy pp. 8 (© Photoshot Holdings Ltd), 10 (© Radius Images), 11 (© Arco Images GmbH), 14 (© Petra Wegner), 17 bottom (© imagebroker), 21 (© Corbis Bridge), 22 (© Paul Collis), 25 (© Kevin Foy); Corbis pp. 5 (© Suzi Eszterhas/Minden Pictures), 7 bottom (© Big Cheese Photo), 15 (© Jim Richardson/National Geographic Society), 23 (© Mike Stotts/ZUMA Press), 24 (© Luo Li/Redlink), 26 (© Alexandra Beier/Reuters), 27 (© Markus Altmann); Getty Images p. 19 (Gerard Brown/Dorling Kindersley); Photoshot pp. 9 (© NHPA/Khalid Ghani), 17 top (© NHPA/Martin Harvey); Shutterstock pp. 4 (© AnetaPics), 7 top (© saipg),12 (© dmvphotos), 13 (© Cynthia Kidwell),18 (© Chris Kruger), 20 (© Johan Swanepoel), 28 (C. Byatt-norman), 29 (© Cynthia Kidwell). Design feature of a dog silhoutte reproduced with permission of Shutterstock (© Cenker Atila).

Cover photograph of a Border collie reproduced with permission of Shutterstock (© Eric Isselée).

Every effort has been made to contact copyright holders of material reproduced in this book. Any omissions will be rectified in subsequent printings if notice is given to the publisher.

Dogs are very intelligent animals. Humans can train dogs to do many different things. Dogs can communicate with each other and some dogs can understand a large number of words and signals from a human. As well as this intelligence, dogs have incredible senses and amazing physical abilities.

Not all dogs live with humans. African wild dogs are one type of dog that lives in the wild.

BEST FRIENDS

Dogs have lived alongside humans for thousands of years. Today, there are around 400 different **breeds** of dog, all of which have particular skills and strengths.

Being a dog

Dogs belong to a group of animals called **mammals**. All mammals have hair or fur on their bodies, feed their young with milk, and have warm blood. Wild dogs live in various parts of the world. In Africa, they live on the grassland called savannah and in woodlands south of the Sahara desert. Wolves live in Asia and parts of North America. A few wolves remain in Europe. Dingoes live in the remote Australian countryside called the outback and an Asian wild dog, called a dhole, lives in south and south-east Asia.

This map shows where different types of wild dog live around the world.

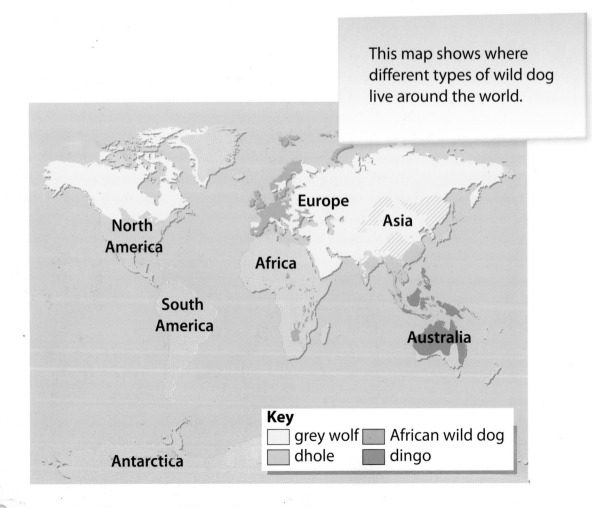

North America

Europe

Asia

Africa

South America

Australia

Antarctica

Key
grey wolf   African wild dog
dhole   dingo

Wolves used to live across most of the northern **hemisphere**. Today, they tend to live in places away from humans.

Dogs that live alongside humans are called **domesticated** dogs. Many dogs are a mixture of different breeds. These mixed-breed dogs are called mongrels. They often have the skills and strengths from a number of breeds. People first started using dogs to guard their homes and **livestock**. Later, dogs were used to help with hunting and herding. Today, people keep dogs for many reasons.

Many dog owners choose a particular breed of dog because it has certain skills or looks.

Dog teamwork

Wild dogs live in groups called packs. They work together as a team to hunt for food. When the dogs in a pack hunt together, they have a much higher chance of catching **prey**. Each dog has a different job to do as the pack tracks prey and surrounds it. The dogs keep chasing their prey until it is too tired to escape. A pack can kill animals much larger than themselves if many dogs attack together.

WOLF FAMILIES

Wolf packs can be made up of as many as 24 wolves, but most have between 6 and 10 members.

African wild dogs work very closely together in a pack.

Wild dogs and wolves share the food they kill with every dog in the pack, not just those involved in the hunt. Sometimes dogs will eat meat and then **regurgitate** some later for members of the pack who weren't at the kill.

These dhole in India have shared the hunt and now feed together.

PACK LIFE

People think domesticated dogs are **descended from** wild wolves or jackals. Domesticated dogs still think like members of a pack. Dog owners train their pet dogs to see them as the pack leader so the dogs will do what their owners say.

Caring for the group

Packs of wild dogs and wolves work together in other ways, too. Often, a few dogs will take turns to watch out for any danger while the rest of the pack rests. Wild dogs and wolves will **groom** each other to keep their fur clean. Many types of wild dog will look after any injured members of the pack, until they are able to hunt again.

Mother wolves lick their pups to keep them clean.

This adult dingo is teaching a pup how to catch a lizard.

HOW DO WE KNOW?

Researchers in Australia have used radio tracking, hidden cameras, and GPS collars fitted to dingoes to get information about how they work together in a pack. The scientists discovered that dingoes train their young to hunt small prey to start with, and gradually teach them to catch larger prey. They also learned that older dingoes teach younger dingoes where the borders of the pack's territory are found.

In a wolf or African wild dog pack, all the adult members will help to take care of the young, which are called pups. After feeding on their mother's milk for about six weeks, wolf pups start to eat regurgitated meat. While the pups are too young to hunt, they are kept together in a safe place where they play while adults protect them.

Dog talk

Dogs can communicate with each other in a number of ways, including barking, whining, growling, and yelping. They also use touch and actions to pass on information to each other. For example, an African wild dog stretches to show the pack that it's time to get up and go hunting. The **dominant** dog in a pack will look at other pack members with a direct stare to show it is in charge. The rest of the dogs in the pack don't usually look straight at each other as this could be seen to be threatening.

Dogs often touch noses when they meet.

A wolf's howl can be heard as far as 16 kilometres (10 miles) away.

HOW DO WE KNOW?

Scientists in Hungary have studied the sounds that dogs make to learn whether dogs can share information with each other. They played recordings of dogs barking in different situations to a number of listening dogs. The scientists discovered that when the listening dogs heard a dog barking for a different reason, their heart rates increased. The listening dogs understood that the dogs were barking for different reasons.

SINGING DOGS

New Guinea dingoes are also called singing dogs because of the howling noise that they make.

Understanding humans

Dogs can be trained to understand a wide range of human words. Researchers think that most dogs can understand around 165 words, as well as gestures and signals from a human. The most intelligent breeds of dog can understand 250 words, as many as a 2½-year-old child.

TOP DOGS

The top five most intelligent breeds of dog are:
1 Border collie
2 Poodle
3 German shepherd
4 Golden retriever
5 Doberman

Many dog owners teach their pet to understand a few basic instructions.

Training

Dogs can be trained to act in certain ways. This ability is called adaptive intelligence. It is different from the powerful senses that give dogs their other great skills and abilities.

Border collies make good sheep dogs because they can follow many different instructions.

HOW DO WE KNOW?

Scientists have studied dogs to see if they can count. The dogs watched researchers lower one treat behind a screen and then another. When the screen was raised, the dogs in the study expected to see the two treats they had watched being put there, and they quickly ate them. But if the researchers secretly added an extra treat or took one way behind the screen, the dogs were surprised when the screen was raised. They stared at the treats for longer, trying to understand. Scientists think dogs can count from one to five.

Dog senses

Dogs' sense of smell is another way in which they communicate with each other. Dogs sniff humans and each other when they meet, and they will remember the way individuals smell. They like to smell the places they pass when they go out on a walk to get information about other animals that have been there. Dogs are able to identify each individual smell around them, even when several are mixed together.

BAD TASTE?

Dogs don't have a very strong sense of taste compared to humans. But this means they're not too fussy about what they eat!

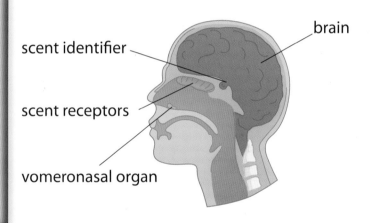

brain

scent identifier

scent receptors

vomeronasal organ

Dogs have much bigger nasal passages than humans and their nasal membrane is packed with scent receptors. A dog also has a large vomeronasal organ in the roof of its mouth. This helps the dog to identify different smells.

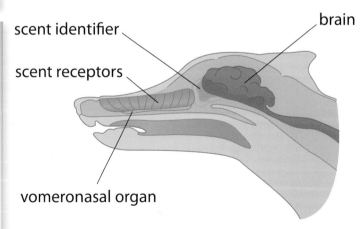

brain

scent identifier

scent receptors

vomeronasal organ

African wild dogs use their strong sense of smell to track prey.

An animal's sense of smell works when scent receptors in its nose detect a smell and its brain identifies it. A human's nose has about five million scent receptors, but a bloodhound is thought to have around 300 million scent receptors! The part of a dog's brain that identifies smells is also about 40 times larger than that part of a human's brain.

Pet puppies use their sense of smell to find out about their world.

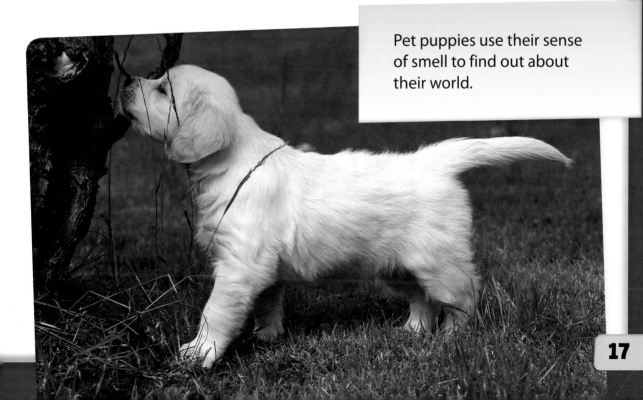

Hearing and sight

Dogs also have a very strong sense of hearing. Different types of dog have different-shaped ears, but all can move their ears to gather sound more effectively. Dogs have 15 muscles in their ears and can move them in all directions and one at a time.

WIDE VIEW

Dogs' sense of sight is better than humans' in dim light. They are not able to see much colour but they can see a wider area because their eyes tend to be further back on the sides of their head than human eyes.

Dogs can hear much higher sounds than humans. In the wild, this means dogs can track small prey such as rabbits and rats, which make squeaking noises.

Dogs' ears are much larger than human ears and they can collect more **sound waves** and hear sounds from further away. Dogs can hear sounds nearly five times as far away from them as humans.

Pet dogs can hear a dog whistle that is too high pitched for their owners to hear.

Find out how humans use dogs' amazing senses to help them on pages 22–27.

Dog emotions

Dogs are able to show basic emotions, such as anger, excitement, and fear. Scientists have even done a study that shows dogs might feel **envy**. Very few animals other than **primates** feel envy. Researchers think that only the most intelligent animals can feel this emotion. It shows that dogs have a certain amount of self-awareness, an important part of intelligence.

Wild dogs show emotions such as anger and fear if they are threatened.

HOW DO WE KNOW?

To prove that dogs can feel envy, scientists carried out an experiment using pairs of dogs. Both dogs were told to do something. When they did it, they were rewarded with a treat. But when one dog got a reward and the other didn't, the dog that hadn't got a treat stopped obeying the instructions. The dogs could see that the humans weren't being fair and reacted by ignoring them!

A wagging tail

Many people believe that when a dog wags its tail, it is happy. In fact, this is a myth! A slow wag can show the dog is unsure about something. A fast wag could mean the dog is excited or that it is feeling aggressive.

Many pet dogs show happiness when they see their owners.

READING EMOTIONS

Some research shows that dogs can understand how humans are feeling by looking at their faces. They can read human emotions such as anger, sadness, or happiness.

Working with dogs

Humans have worked with dogs for thousands of years. Different dog breeds developed because people wanted dogs with particular strengths and abilities. Some breeds of dog learn especially quickly and can be trained to help humans in different ways.

Humans have used dogs to guard their property for thousands of years. Good guard dogs can sniff out a stranger very quickly.

HELPFUL HUSKIES

Chukchi people living in the Arctic first trained teams of huskies to pull sledges across the ice. They also used huskies as guard dogs.

Hunting and herding

People still use dogs to help them hunt and herd other animals. Some dogs use their sense of smell to sniff out and track prey. Pointers use their noses to show their owner in what direction they will find prey. Others fetch prey that has already been shot. Terriers can run down into burrows or dig out pests such as rats and rabbits.

Dogs work on cattle ranches all around the world.

Dogs that are used to herd livestock, such as Australian cattle dogs and Border collies, can understand a large number of words, whistled instructions, and hand gestures. They need to be very intelligent and strong. The dogs move herds by moving around them, barking, and nipping at their feet.

Sniffer dogs

People are able to use dogs' incredible sense of smell to help them in many different ways. The police have used dogs for a long time. German shepherd dogs are often used as patrol dogs because these strong, fast dogs can easily chase and stop criminals. If the police are searching for a criminal or a missing person, an officer can give a police dog a piece of that person's clothing or belongings to smell. The police dog can then track the scent and try to find the person.

This police dog is being trained to catch criminals.

Sniffer dogs often work at stations and airports.

Other police dogs are trained to recognize the smell of illegal drugs or bombs. These sniffer dogs are able to find the scents of these things even when they are hidden by other smells.

DETECTING CANCER

There have been studies to see whether dogs can be specially trained to sniff people's breath to tell if they have cancer. Scientists have tried to create a machine to do this, too, but nothing as accurate as a dog has been built so far.

Search and rescue dogs

Search dogs find people who are missing or trapped after disasters such as earthquakes or vehicle crashes. They smell the air and track people's scents until they find them. These dogs can work in the dark and also use their sense of hearing to find people. Dogs can pick up the smell of a human from 500 metres (545 yards) away.

Rescue dogs can find people buried under snow.

BIG DOG

Big Dog is a robot dog that has been made to work in difficult **terrain**. The robot can walk, run, climb, and carry heavy loads, and has a built-in GPS system to tell it where to go.

Guide dogs help their owners to move around safely.

Guide dogs

Guide dogs help people who have difficulty seeing or hearing. When the dogs are still puppies, they are trained to get used to people and the world around them. They learn to walk ahead of their owner and stop at kerbs. They also learn to obey important commands and to judge space so their owner doesn't bump into things.

Therapy dogs

Therapy dogs are good-natured dogs that are trained to work with people who are ill or have had an upsetting experience. They allow people to stroke and cuddle them for comfort.

The amazing dog

Many people love the company of dogs, and enjoy living or working alongside them. This is largely because of dogs' intelligence and ability to respond to and help humans in their daily lives. Dogs can be trained to do many different things. This ability, along with their physical strength and incredible senses, makes them truly amazing animals.

Young dogs are often keen to learn new skills.

Dog superpowers

You're already pretty good at understanding instructions and showing other people when you're happy or sad. But what would be best about being a dog?

- If you could work in a team like a wolf or an African wild dog, nobody could beat you!

- If you could sniff out all the different smells around you from half a kilometre away, you could easily find the chocolate your mum has hidden!

- If you could turn your ears around, you'd be able to hear the quietest sound on the other side of the playground!

- If you had the running speed of a dog, you could chase criminals and catch them for the police!

As these wolf pups play, they are learning things they will need to know when they are adults.

Glossary

breed term used for group of animals within a domesticated species. For example, a Doberman is a breed of dog.

descended from originally came from another species

domesticated trained to live and work with humans

dominant having the most power and control

envy jealousy; wanting what someone else has

GPS global positioning system; system that uses satellites in space to follow movement on Earth

groom clean the fur or skin

hemisphere northern or southern half of Earth

livestock animals kept on a farm

mammal type of warm-blooded animal that has a backbone, feeds on its mother's milk when young, and has hair on its body

prey animal that is eaten by other animals

primate one of the orders (groups) that mammals are divided into. Apes, monkeys, and humans are all primates.

regurgitate bring up food that has been swallowed, back into the mouth

sound wave wave that carries sound through the air

terrain shape and features of the land

Find out more

Books

Dogs (Animal Family Albums), Paul Mason (Raintree, 2013)

Dogs, Kathryn Walker (Wayland, 2007)

Dogs, Sally Morgan (Franklin Watts, 2011)

My Dog is a Hero, Rebecca Camerena (Scholastic, 2012)

Websites

www.bbc.co.uk/nature/life/African_Wild_Dog

Find out about different types of wild dog on the BBC's website.

www.guidedogs.org.uk

Visit the Guide Dogs website to learn more about how dogs are trained to help visually impaired people.

www.rspca.org.uk/allaboutanimals/pets/dogs

The RSPCA website has plenty of information about looking after dogs as well as many interesting facts.

Place to visit

Paws for Thought Dog Display Team

www.pawsforthought-dogdisplay.co.uk/index.htm

Find out when this dog display team is performing in your area and go and see them in action!

Index